IMAGES
of America

NORTHERN KENTUCKY'S DIXIE HIGHWAY

Page Ten THE DIXIE HIGHWAY May, 1924

Only Official Routing of Dixie Highway—Eastern Branch

EASTERN BRANCH

Sault Ste. Marie, Mich., to Mackinaw		65 Miles
Macinaw to Alpena		119 Miles
Alpena to Bay City		137 Miles
Bay City to Bad Axe	79 Miles	
Bad Axe to Port Huron	63 Miles	
Port Huron to Algonac	25 Miles	
Algonac to Detroit	46 Miles	
	213 Miles	
Bay City to Saginaw		16 Miles
Saginaw to Detroit		95 Miles
Detroit to Toledo		61 Miles
Toledo, Ohio, to Lima		78 Miles
Lima to Dayton		74 Miles
Dayton to Cincinnati		61 Miles
Cincinnati, Ohio, to Lexington (via Georgetown)		85 Miles
Via Cynthiana, Ky.	96 Miles	
Lexington, Ky., to Mt. Vernon		63 Miles
Mt. Vernon to Jellico		83 Miles
Jellico to Knoxville		72 Miles
Knoxville, Tenn., to Chattanooga		132 Miles
Chattanooga to Atlanta (via Dalton)		126 Miles
Atlanta, Ga., to Macon		95 Miles
Macon to Waycross		172 Miles
Waycross to Jacksonville		77 Miles
Jacksonville, Fla., to St. Augustine		41 Miles
St. Augustine to Daytona		73 Miles
Daytona to West Palm Beach		195 Miles
West Palm Beach to Miami, Fla.		67 Miles
Total		1987 Miles

WESTERN BRANCH

Sault Ste. Marie, Mich., to Mackinaw		65 Miles
Mackinaw to Petosky		38 Miles
Petosky to Traverse City		72 Miles
Traverse City to Manistee		67 Miles
Manistee to Muskegon		94 Miles
Muskegon to Grand Haven		13 Miles
Grand Haven to South Haven	54 Miles	
South Haven to St. Joseph	30 Miles	
St. Joseph to Niles	24 Miles	
	108 Miles	
Grand Haven to Grand Rapids		32 Miles
Grand Rapids to Kalamazoo		50 Miles
Kalamazoo to Niles		59 Miles
Niles to South Bend		11 Miles
South Bend to Indianapolis		139 Miles
(Via Logansport-Michigantown)		
Indianapolis to Paoli		99 Miles
Paoli to Louisville		49 Miles
Louisville to Horse Cave		84 Miles
(Horse Cave to Mammoth Cave)	14.4 Miles	
Horse Cave to Bowling Green		35 Miles
Bowling Green to Springfield		43 Miles
Springfield to Nashville		30 Miles
Nashville to Chattanooga		160 Miles
Chattanooga to Atlanta (via Rome)		139 Miles
Atlanta to Macon		95 Miles
Macon to Thomasville		167 Miles
Thomasville to Tallahassee		35 Miles
Tallahassee to Gainesville		162 Miles
Gainesville to Ocala		44 Miles
Ocala to Orlando		88 Miles
Orlando to Haines City		40 Miles
Haines City to Fort Myers		147 Miles
Fort Myers to Marco, Fla.		50 Miles
Total		2107 Miles

CHICAGO TO INDIANAPOLIS-DAYTON, OHIO

Chicago to Danville	135 Miles
Danville to Crawfordsville	41 Miles
Crawfordsville to Indianapolis	45 Miles
Indianapolis, Ind., to Dayton, Ohio	108 Miles
Total	329 Miles

This official map of Dixie Highway appeared in the *Dixie Highway* magazine in May 1924. The photographs in this book were taken along the Eastern Branch, as it runs from Covington, Kentucky, through Florence, Kentucky, via U.S. 25. (Courtesy of Amy Gillis Lowry and Abbie Tucker Parks, authors of *North Georgia's Dixie Highway*.)

ON THE COVER: A genuine 20-horse team pulls this obelisk from the quarry in Covington up Dixie Highway for delivery to Highland Cemetery in Fort Mitchell in this 1893 photograph. Delivery of such a large tombstone monument called for not only horsepower, but a considerable amount of manpower, as well. (Courtesy of Chester F. Geaslen.)

IMAGES
of America

NORTHERN KENTUCKY'S DIXIE HIGHWAY

Deborah Kohl Kremer

ARCADIA
PUBLISHING

ISBN 978-0-7385-6773-0

Published by Arcadia Publishing
Charleston, South Carolina

Printed in the United States of America

Library of Congress Control Number: 2009924096

For all general information contact Arcadia Publishing at:
Telephone 843-853-2070
Fax 843-853-0044
E-mail sales@arcadiapublishing.com
For customer service and orders:
Toll-Free 1-888-313-2665

Visit us on the Internet at www.arcadiapublishing.com

I dedicate this book to my grandpa, Chester F. Geaslen, who taught Northern Kentucky how to Stroll Along Memory Lane.

Contents

Acknowledgments

A book like this certainly cannot be completed alone. I had to depend on the help of so many generous individuals who invited me to their homes and shared their precious photographs with me. I have been in basements, garages, and archives and sifted through boxes and albums, searching for these photographs. I certainly want to give credit to those people who shared with me. After each photograph, you will see a credit to the person who so generously supplied me with the photograph as well as information about it. And to those people, I say thanks. But I also owe a debt of gratitude to the people who connected me to the photograph owner; they deserve credit, too. So the following people are those who helped me make these connections, those who tried to find photographs and/or connections for me, and those who helped me get my facts straight. I hope they accept my sincere thanks: Sr. Mary Joan Terese Niklas, Sisters of Notre Dame; Bridget Striker; Michael Embry; Pam Ciafardini Casebolt; Dave Schroeder; Jeannine Kreinbrink; Paul Tenkotte; Mary Pat Lewis; Kevin Howland; Jimmy Kidd; Jeff Kramer; Nancy Goetz Barton; Scott and Cathy Ringo; Geri King; Alex Freihofer; Jerry Hoffman; Drew Hoffman; Ken Kallmeyer; Tiffany and Jeanne Pangallo; Maggie McLeod; Rae Wise; Connie Fry; Cam Fry; Betty Dietz; Ben Krumpelman; Kathy Geaslen; Warren and Sis Heist; Lee and Eileen Hartke; Jim Reis; Terry and Julie Kremer Bricking; the waitresses at Colonial Cottage Restaurant; and my editor at Arcadia Publishing, Luke Cunningham.

I also have to pay respects to my family, who helped in so many ways. First I have to thank my grandfather, local historian Chester F. Geaslen. Although he has been gone for many years, he was still able to lead me to many photographs. My parents, Paul and Peg Kohl, are the greatest. Dad's ability to identify the make, model, and year of a car just by looking at its bumper really came in handy. Mom, who has no problem calling someone she has not seen in 50 years, made the calls and spread the word about this book, which led to many successful photographs. My sister, Nancy Hoffman, who seems to know most people in Northern Kentucky, connected me to many people I would have never found on my own. And mostly, I have to thank my husband, Nick, who listened to my endless stories about these photographs and encouraged me to write this book. And of course, thanks to my children, Ellie and Paul, the best kids a mom could have. Love you all.

Introduction

While much has been written about the Dixie Highway in regard to its national importance, this book shows the profound effects from just a sliver of it. This little stretch, just the 15 miles or so from Covington through Florence, Kentucky, brought life to so many people. Although it only takes about 20 minutes to drive that length today, the sights along the way have changed, in some instances several times. Hopefully these photographs will bring back some memories or just explain how things got to be the way they are now.

The original path was thought to be created from a buffalo trace; as the buffalo migrated through the area, they actually started to form roads. So when people finally got to this area, the paths were already created. Then as people started migrating themselves, away from the downtown area, they followed this path, which was charted "US Highway Number 25" in 1819. This dirt road served as the main north-south corridor in the area, dubbed the Covington-Lexington Turnpike. There was much celebration when it was chosen as the route for the Dixie Highway, which would be a paved road running from Sault Ste. Marie, Michigan, to Miami, Florida.

The Dixie Highway was completed in the early 1920s, but it was still called the Lexington Pike for years to come. Northern Kentucky's slice of the Dixie goes by many names. In the Covington area, it is known as Pike Street, but it is also known as U.S. 25, U.S. 42, and U.S. 127. People living in the area in the 1930s, 1940s, and 1950s also referred to it as the Gourmet Strip, as it was widely known for the fine dining establishments that dotted the route.

Northern Kentucky's portion of the Dixie Highway was the lifeblood of the small communities along the way. Although the railroad can also be credited with the development of some towns south of Covington, it was the Dixie Highway that supported the shops, taverns, and motels and helped the communities thrive. This book will take you through these communities, with some photographs dating back to the mid-1800s and some from as recently as the 1980s. We start the book on the western tip of Covington, as Dixie Highway, which is known as Pike Street through there, leaves the city and heads up the big hill and around the bend into the suburbs.

The city of Park Hills was a sleepy area with just a few homes that really benefitted with the paving of the Dixie Highway. The city's hilly terrain was unsuitable for farming, so Park Hills was basically inactive as surrounding communities began to prosper with the arrival of farmers and residents. But with the popularity of the car, and the paving of the Dixie Highway, many notable restaurants began to spring up along the route. These fine dining establishments and the construction of homes just off the Dixie Highway really gave Park Hills the anchors it needed to flourish.

Straddling Dixie Highway between Park Hills and Fort Mitchell was the city of Lookout Heights, which is now a part of Fort Wright. This area of the city sits high atop a hill, which (hence the name) provided a good lookout to the cities of Covington and Cincinnati below.

Fort Mitchell, which was named after a Civil War fort within the city, was incorporated in 1910. Wealthy people, who presumably were looking to get away from city life, began building large homes just off Dixie Highway, near the border with Fort Wright. In 1927, the residents who lived farther down Dixie Highway, near the streetcar "end of the line," incorporated their town into the city of South Fort Mitchell. In 1966, the cities voted to become one and the name Fort Mitchell was embraced by both.

Lakeside Park, although mostly residential, also ties its origins to Dixie Highway. Incorporated as a city in 1930, it grew to be an area of fine homes on streets that sprouted off the original Lexington Turnpike.

Farther southward, Crestview Hills was mainly farmland that began taking root in the early 1920s. Original residents built their stately homes right along the highway or in the first subdivision in the city, which was near the Edgewood border.

The city of Edgewood, formed in 1948, grew primarily from its ties to Dudley Road. There is a small strip, less than a mile long, where the Dixie Highway runs through Edgewood. This speck of the much larger city runs from the intersection of Dudley Road and Dixie Highway to just past Lyndale Road.

The community of Erlanger ties its roots to both the Lexington Turnpike and the arrival of the Southern Railroad. A train depot was built in the city in 1877, and it served as a welcome mat for many travelers. But it was the residents of Erlanger who depended upon the Dixie Highway and focused their town around it. Merchants, banks, hotels, churches, and restaurants hung out their shingle and gave Erlanger an actual downtown.

The city of Elsmere, which was known as South Erlanger until it incorporated in 1896, has a history similar to that of Erlanger. The old stagecoach route that is now Dixie Highway runs right through the city. The arrival of the Southern Railroad, running from New Orleans to Cincinnati, had regular stops at Woodside Park, a popular picnic spot in Elsmere, which put it on the map.

Florence, incorporated in 1830, was originally known as the town of Crossroads. The original name still seems to fit as it is the site of many converging routes. Although the Dixie Highway is made up of U.S. 25 and U.S. 42 through most of Northern Kentucky, it is in Florence where it splits apart—or merges together, depending on your direction. Although Main Street in Florence was the central business district for decades, it was the connection of Main Street to the Lexington Turnpike that is credited with its growth.

This outward growth of a downtown is today known as urban sprawl. Our ancestors certainly did not need a fancy name for laying their stakes, building their homes, and protecting their livelihood. Whether these people were farmers, shopkeepers, restaurateurs, or commuters, they laid the groundwork for these fine suburban communities we have today. Each of these communities has their own personality and history. While outsiders may just assume that traveling from Covington through Florence along the Dixie Highway is all just a blur of tiny towns, residents know where each one stops and a new one starts and value each one.

One

Around the Big Bend

From Covington into Park Hills

Standing stately at 627 Pike Street is St. John's Catholic Church. (Courtesy of the Covington Province of the Sisters of Notre Dame.)

Frank Krumpelmann's ice truck was a familiar sight as he delivered ice in Covington and along Dixie Highway, as seen in the early 1900s. (Courtesy of Mary Downey and Beverly Landrum-McIntosh.)

This 1950 photograph is looking south on what is called both Dixie Highway and Pike Street. The streetcar rounds the bend and starts climbing the hill to Park Hills. (Courtesy of Earl Abeln.)

This aerial view, which was taken in the 1970s, shows the big bend in the road near 718 Pike Street. (Courtesy of the Boehmker family.)

The intersection of U.S. 25 and Montague Street, looking north, is seen in this 1970s photograph. (Courtesy of the Boehmker family.)

Henry Boehmker, who was known as Heine, opened Heine's Café at 718 Pike Street in 1939. He stands in front with his granddaughter in this early-1940s photograph. (Courtesy of the Boehmker family.)

Henry ("Heine") and Marie Boehmker stand in front of Heine's Café at 718 Pike Street on May 20, 1945. There was also a barbershop in the building; notice the familiar barber pole. (Courtesy of the Boehmker family.)

Ruth Boehmker Fedders and a cute little girl pose in front of Heine's Café in this image looking north. (Courtesy of the Boehmker family.)

Sophie Walz and her daughter Emma Rachel Walz stand outside their home at 1101 Pike Street, at the corner of Pike and Montague Streets, in this photograph taken in 1900. (Courtesy of Earl and Georgiana Walz.)

This picture looks southbound on Dixie Highway near the Covington–Park Hills border. Notice the "Al Smith for President" bumper sticker. Smith ran an unsuccessful campaign for president in 1928. He was defeated by Herbert Hoover. (Courtesy of the Covington Province of the Sisters of Notre Dame.)

Mrs. Hahn (third from left), owner of the Hahn Hotel, is seen here in front of the hotel in this 1961 photograph. The other ladies are unidentified. (Courtesy of Tom Stamm, Fort Mitchell Garage.)

Looking northbound on the Dixie Highway near the Covington–Park Hills border is this photograph from the late 1920s. (Courtesy of the Covington Province of the Sisters of Notre Dame.)

The Hahn Hotel, at 1424 Dixie Highway, was torn down in the early 1970s. (Courtesy of Tom Stamm, Fort Mitchell Garage.)

The Hahn Hotel, seen in these 1960 photographs, was located at 1424 Dixie Highway. It was frequented by tourists, but today it might be called an "extended stay hotel," as some people stayed for quite a while. (Courtesy of Tom Stamm, Fort Mitchell Garage.)

Fort Mitchell Garage stood at 1420 Dixie Highway in 1975. (Courtesy of Tom Stamm, Fort Mitchell Garage.)

On the back of this postcard of Den Lou Motel, at 1430 Dixie Highway, it says, "In the center of Northern Kentucky's Finest Restaurants. Three minutes from downtown Cincinnati. Air Conditioning, Tile Baths, Phones, TV and Hot Water Heat." (Courtesy of Tom Stamm, Fort Mitchell Garage.)

Looking south on Dixie Highway, one can see the Shell station that stood at 1430 Dixie Highway. (Courtesy of Tom Stamm, Fort Mitchell Garage.)

The same Shell station is seen in this 1940 photograph looking toward the north. (Courtesy of Tom Stamm, Fort Mitchell Garage.)

White Horse Tavern at 1501 Dixie Highway opened in 1936. Everyone loved the giant white Thoroughbred on the roof and the upscale dining offered inside. The restaurant burned down in the early 1970s. (Courtesy of the Kenton County Public Library, Covington, Kentucky.)

Tom Stamm stands in front of his business, Stamm Brothers Garage, at 1420 Dixie Highway. He changed the name to Fort Mitchell Garage right before opening in 1973. Notice the Den Lou Motel in the background and the motel sign still standing from the former Hahn Hotel. (Courtesy of Tom Stamm, Fort Mitchell Garage.)

Kremer Farm, located near 1600 Dixie Highway, is shown here. Matt Kremer (left) and his brother Nick Kremer pose with their horses in the early 1900s. (Courtesy of Julie Kremer.)

Matt Kremer (third from left) is pictured with friends at the Kremer Farm, located near 1600 Dixie Highway, in this early-1900s photograph. (Courtesy of Julie Kremer.)

Minnie Kremer stands with her favorite Jersey cow, named Daisy, at the Kremer Farm near 1600 Dixie Highway. This photograph was taken in the early 1900s. (Courtesy of Julie Kremer.)

This truck from Fort Mitchell Garage was a familiar sight along Dixie Highway in the mid-1960s. (Courtesy of Tom Stamm, Fort Mitchell Garage.)

St. Joseph Heights, which is the home of the Covington Province of the Sisters of Notre Dame, was completed in 1927. The grand building at 1601 Dixie Highway must have just been completed in this photograph, as there is no landscaping or grass planted yet. (Courtesy of the Covington Province of the Sisters of Notre Dame.)

This 1910 postcard shows the first property of the Sisters of Notre Dame, which was at the corner of St. Joseph Lane and Dixie Highway. (Courtesy of the Covington Province of the Sisters of Notre Dame.)

This is an aerial view of St. Joseph Heights at 1601 Dixie Highway. At the bottom of the photograph is Dixie Highway; upper left are the sisters' cemetery and some homes on St. Joseph Lane. (Courtesy of the Covington Province of the Sisters of Notre Dame.)

An aerial view of 1420 Dixie Highway includes the Den Lou Motel on the left and Fort Mitchell Garage on the right. In the background can be seen the old Park Hills School. (Courtesy of Tom Stamm, Fort Mitchell Garage.)

These girls stand on the hillside in front of St. Joseph Heights at 1601 Dixie Highway in the early 1930s. It appears that the Sisters of Notre Dame were having a large gathering, perhaps a picnic for the sisters' families, which was common at the time. (Courtesy of the Covington Province of the Sisters of Notre Dame.)

Here is a late-1940s or early-1950s gathering at St. Joseph Heights. (Courtesy of the Covington Province of the Sisters of Notre Dame.)

The Blue Star Tavern at 1622 Dixie Highway opened in 1936. They changed the name to Town and Country in 1950. (Courtesy of Behringer-Crawford Museum.)

The Blue Star Tavern was a comfortable restaurant known throughout the region for their good food and warm service. Owners Carl and Olga Wooton were always on hand to welcome their guests and knew most by name. With their varied menu options, from "Golden Fried Frog Legs" to the "Mammoth Cave Special," which was a fried ham sandwich, to the double-decker baked pork and tomato sandwich, customers knew they were in for a treat. (Courtesy of Julie Kremer.)

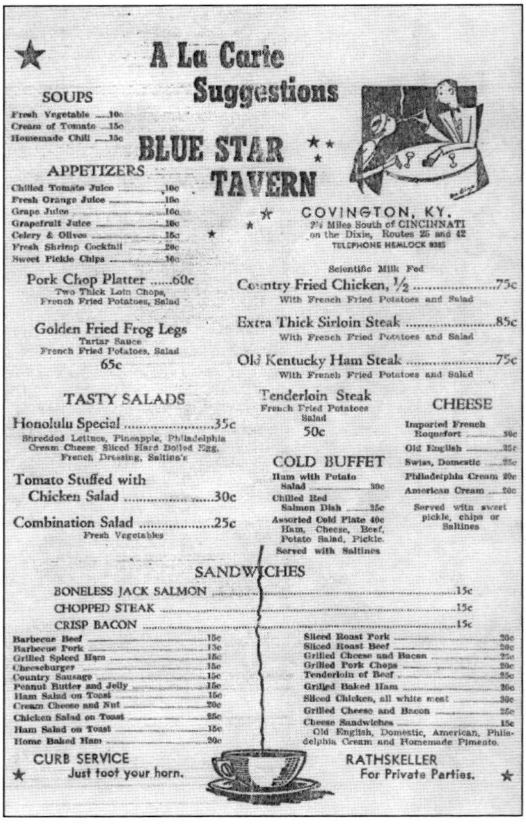

A La Carte Suggestions

BLUE STAR TAVERN

COVINGTON, KY.
2¼ Miles South of CINCINNATI
on the Dixie, Routes 25 and 42
TELEPHONE HEMLOCK 9385

SOUPS

Fresh Vegetable 10c
Cream of Tomato 15c
Homemade Chili 15c

APPETIZERS

Chilled Tomato Juice 10c
Fresh Orange Juice 10c
Grape Juice 10c
Grapefruit Juice 10c
Celery & Olives 15c
Fresh Shrimp Cocktail 20c
Sweet Pickle Chips 10c

Pork Chop Platter 60c
Two Thick Loin Chops, French Fried Potatoes, Salad

Golden Fried Frog Legs
Tartar Sauce
French Fried Potatoes, Salad
65c

Scientific Milk Fed
Country Fried Chicken, ½ 75c
With French Fried Potatoes and Salad

Extra Thick Sirloin Steak 85c
With French Fried Potatoes and Salad

Old Kentucky Ham Steak 75c
With French Fried Potatoes and Salad

TASTY SALADS

Honolulu Special 35c
Shredded Lettuce, Pineapple, Philadelphia Cream Cheese Sliced Hard Boiled Egg, French Dressing, Saltina's

Tomato Stuffed with Chicken Salad 30c

Combination Salad 25c
Fresh Vegetables

Tenderloin Steak
French Fried Potatoes
Salad
50c

COLD BUFFET

Ham with Potato Salad 30c
Chilled Red Salmon Dish 25c
Assorted Cold Plate 40c
Ham, Cheese, Beef, Potato Salad, Pickle.
Served with Saltines

CHEESE

Imported French Roquefort 30c
Old English 25c
Swiss, Domestic 25c
Philadelphia Cream 20c
American Cream 20c
Served with sweet pickle, chips or Saltines

SANDWICHES

BONELESS JACK SALMON 15c
CHOPPED STEAK 15c
CRISP BACON 15c

Barbecue Beef 15c
Barbecue Pork 15c
Grilled Spiced Ham 15c
Cheeseburger 15c
Country Sausage 15c
Peanut Butter and Jelly 15c
Ham Salad on Toast 15c
Cream Cheese and Nut 20c
Chicken Salad on Toast 25c
Ham Salad on Toast 15c
Home Baked Ham 30c

Sliced Roast Pork 20c
Sliced Roast Beef 20c
Grilled Cheese and Bacon 25c
Grilled Pork Chops 20c
Tenderloin of Beef 25c
Grilled Baked Ham 20c
Sliced Chicken, all white meat 30c
Grilled Cheese and Bacon 25c
Cheese Sandwiches 15c
Old English, Domestic, American, Philadelphia Cream and Homemade Pimento.

CURB SERVICE
Just toot your horn.

RATHSKELLER
For Private Parties.

COCKTAILS & ASSORTED DRINKS

MANHATTAN 25c
(Bourbon, Bitters, Vermouth)
MARTINI 25c
(Gin, Vermouth, Bitters, Olive)
OLD FASHION 25c
(Bourbon, Bitters, Fruit)
TOM COLLINS 25c
(Gin, Lemon, Sugar, Fruit)
WHISKEY SOUR 25c
(Bourbon, Lemon, Sugar, Fruit)
ALEXANDER 25c
(Gin, Creme de Cocao, Cream)
BACARDI 35c
(Bacardi, Grenadine, Lime)
PINK LADY 25c
(Gin, Grenadine, Lime, Cream)
SLOE GIN FIZZ 30c
(Sloe Gin, White Egg, Lemon, Sugar)
DAIQUIRI 35c
(Rum, Lime, Sugar)
SIDE CAR 35c
(Brandy, Cointreau, Lemon)
CUBA LIBRE 35c
(Rum, Coca Cola, Lime)
GIN RICKEY 25c
(Gin, Lime, Seltzer)
CHAMPAGNE 50c
(Champagne, Bitters, Fruit)
SINGAPORE SLING 35c
(Brandy, Gin, Lime, Benedictine)
EGG NOGG 35c
(Bourbon, Egg, Sugar, Milk)

High Balls 5c Extra

BOURBON WHISKEY

OLD CHARTER, 4 year 25c
BOND & LILLARD, 4 year 25c
BOURBON SPRINGS, 3½ year 20c
SEAGRAM'S 7 CROWN 20c
T. W. SAMUELS, 2 year 15c
KENTUCKY TAVERN, 4 year 25c
OLD TAYLOR, 4 year 25c
OLD GRANDAD, 4 year 25c
FOUR ROSES, blended 25c
LEWIS HUNTER, 3 year 15c
OLD OVERHOLT, bonded 25c

RYE WHISKEY

OLD OVERHOLT, bonded 25c

CANADIAN BONDED

Seagram's V. O. 25c
Canadian Club 25c

SCOTCH

White Horse 30c
Johnny Walker, red 30c
Black & White 30c
Vat 69 .... 30c
Haig & Haig, pinch 40c
Cutty Sark 40c

RUM

Bacardi Rum 30c
Rico 25c

BRANDY

3 Star Hennessey 35c
Martell 35c
Apple Jack 25c
Apricot 25c

LIQUORS & CORDIALS

Benedictine 35c
Creme De Cacao 40c
Cointreau 35c
Rock & Rye 15c
Cherry 35c

WINES

SHERRY 15c
MUSCATEL 15c

CHAMPAGNE, Split $1.00

Their cocktail menu at the Blue Star Tavern was as diverse as their dinner menu, featuring drinks like the Sloe Gin Fizz, the Singapore Sling, and Egg Nogg. (Courtesy of Julie Kremer.)

★ WOOTON'S BLUE STAR FEATURES ★

SANDWICHES

Blue Star Special 15c
CHOPPED STEAK—Top Grade Steak, chopped and broiled. Served on Toasted Buttered Bun with Our Famous Sauce

Double Chopped Steak 25c
Deliciously Different

Mammouth Cave Special 30c
Old Kentucky Ham, Fried

Virginia Beach Special 15c
Grilled Franks, Crisp Bacon

Kentucky Special 50c
½ Chicken, Country Fried

SALADS

With Choice of Dressings

Sliced Tomatoes 15c
Potato Salad 15c
Cottage Cheese 15c
Hawaiian 25c
Assorted Fruit 25c
Fresh Shrimp 35c
Lettuce and Tomato 20c
Head Lettuce 15c

After Theatre Specials . .

BONELESS FISH SDW. ....15¢

SHRIMP SALAD wafers....35¢

COLD PLATE......35¢
(ham & potato salad)

//////////////////

RUM COLA......25¢ ★

Beer in Bottles

Bavarian 10c
Hudepohl 10c
Wiedemann's 10c
Pabst in Cans 15c
Budweiser 15c
Barbarossa 15c
Carlings Ale 15c

Beverages

Pure Orange Juice .. 10c
Orangeade 10c
Lemonade 10c
Welch's Grape Juice 10c
Tomato Juice 10c
Coffee 5c
Milk Shake 15c
Tea, individual pot 10c
Milk 5c
Chocolate Milk .. 5 & 10c
Buttermilk .... 5 & 10c
Hot Chocolate 10c
Coca Cola
In bottles 10c
Glass 5c
Malted Milk 20c
Vichy, Glass 5c
Bottle 10c

TOASTED DOUBLE DECKERS

1. CLUB SANDWICH 30c
Chicken, Bacon and Tomato
2. SLICED CHICKEN (white meat) 35c
Chicken and Tomato
3. HAM AND BEEF 30c
4. HAM AND HARDBOILED EGG 25c
5. BAKED PORK AND TOMATO 25c
6. CRISP BACON AND TOMATO 25c
7. HAM AND CHEESE 25c
8. BAKED HAM AND TOMATO 25c
9. CHOPPED STEAK AND CHEESE 25c

Lettuce and Mayonnaise included on all Double Deckers

PLEASE NOTE . . . Only Grade "A" Meats and other Food Products of the Highest Quality are used at the Blue Star. . . . Olga and Carl Wooton

Frank Foltz (right) is pictured in front of his farm on Dixie Highway in the early 1900s. (Courtesy of Judy Foltz Whelan.)

St. John's Catholic Church is shown in this postcard celebrating the church's centennial year. The church on the right was established in 1848 and was originally located at Leonard and Worth Streets in Covington. The Diocese of Covington built the new church on the left in 1924. (Courtesy of Raymond and Jean Schmitz.)

This Golden Jubilee Mass of Reverend Monsignor Henry Hanses on June 14, 1969, took place at St. John's Catholic Church. (Courtesy of the Covington Province of the Sisters of Notre Dame.)

The St. John School at 625 Pike Street was established in the 1920s. In the 1980s, the school consolidated with St. James, St. Boniface, Mother of God, and St. Ann Schools and changed its name to Prince of Peace. (Courtesy of the Covington Province of the Sisters of Notre Dame.)

Two

The Suburbs
Fort Wright and Fort Mitchell

This tollgate was near the intersection of Dixie Highway and Kyles Lane. The photograph, which dates back to the dawn of the 20th century, shows gate operator Bob Willis and his wife chatting with a milkman who has just paid his toll. (Courtesy Chester F. Geaslen.)

Here is an aerial view of Fort Wright, near the intersection of Dixie Highway and Kyles Lane. (Courtesy of Dean Russell and the City of Fort Wright.)

Henry Oelsner shows off his Civil War gun, which was called a goose gun or a Blunder bus gun, in this 1860s-era photograph. He is standing near 1665 Dixie Highway in Fort Wright. (Courtesy of Nancy Oelsner Baute.)

Schlosser Fish was known around the world for its giant goldfish, which are now known as koi. This photograph, which was taken around the beginning of the 20th century, shows the business, located on the east side of Dixie Highway near Kyles Lane. (Courtesy Nancy Oelsner Baute.)

Eugene Schlosser raised trotting horses and goldfish on his property near 1665 Dixie Highway. He is shown here with his dogs in 1927. (Courtesy of Nancy Oelsner Baute.)

Dixie Gardens Drive-In at 1665 Dixie Highway opened on July 3, 1947, with a 100-foot-tall screen, parking for 700, and the movie *Three Little Girls in Blue*. In 1949, the drive-in started its annual Easter Egg Hunt for children; one lucky grand prize winner was awarded a pony. The drive-in faced controversy over the years because the screen faced I-75, and it was blamed for traffic accidents when some of the steamier movies of the 1970s were showing. Although the Dixie Gardens charged a per-passenger price for each car, the attendants rarely checked trunks for stowaways. Local teens knew where to locate the well-worn sneak-in trail through the woods on the north side of the theater. The screen burned in 1990, and the drive-in never reopened. (Above, courtesy of Dean Russell and the City of Fort Wright; below, courtesy of Todd Kruempelman.)

St. Agnes Chapel, at 1680 Dixie Highway, was built in 1930. It was considered a chapel of St. Mary's Cathedral in Covington. The original structure was a Sears and Roebuck church, as it was ordered from the catalog and built from a kit. (Courtesy of Ed and Carol Whitehead.)

The interior of the St. Agnes Chapel is shown on this postcard. (Courtesy of the Covington Province of the Sisters of Notre Dame.)

The Fort Wright and Lookout Heights areas grew rapidly, and St. Agnes, originally part of St. Mary's Cathedral in Covington, was declared a church with its own parish in 1954. (Courtesy of the Covington Province of the Sisters of Notre Dame.)

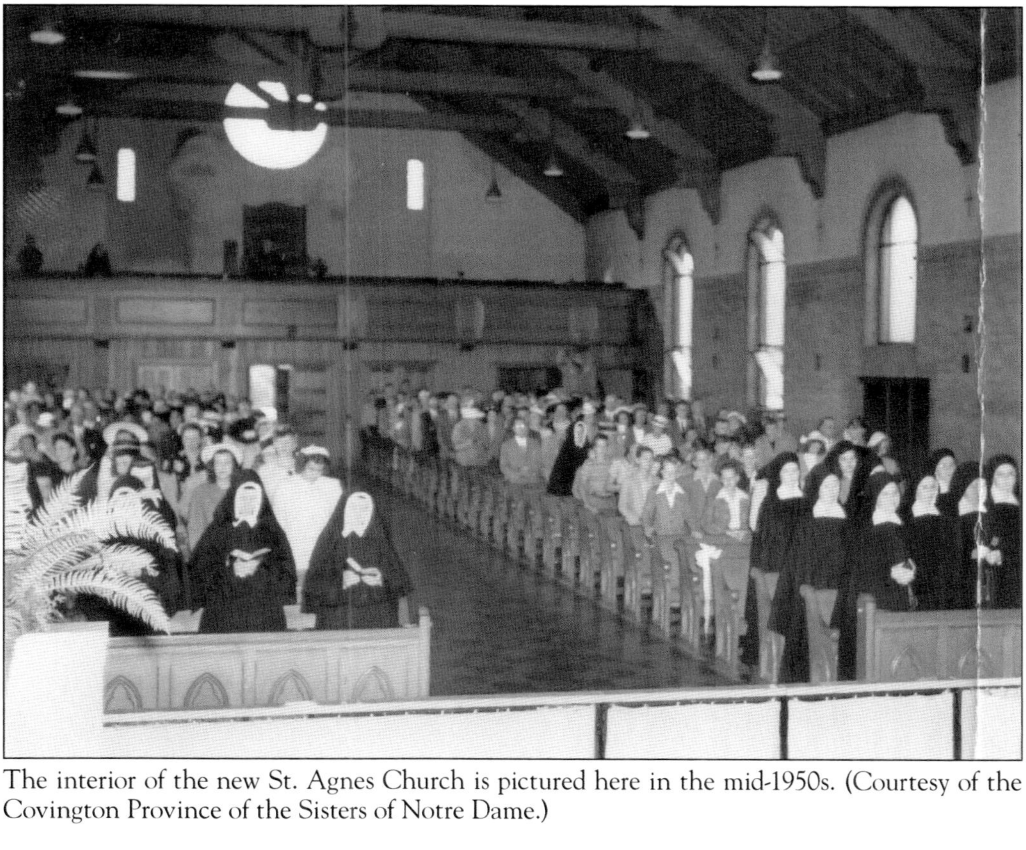

The interior of the new St. Agnes Church is pictured here in the mid-1950s. (Courtesy of the Covington Province of the Sisters of Notre Dame.)

Jimmy Brink's Lookout House at 1721 Dixie Highway was photographed in the late 1950s. The business, originally known as Rush's Tavern, was founded in the 1850s. It had a high cupola on the roof that was used as a lookout. By the 1880s, the tavern was simply known as the Lookout House. (Courtesy of Fred Hellmann.)

In this *c.* 1952 aerial view of Dixie Highway in Fort Wright, notice the Lookout House in the center and St. Agnes Church in the upper right corner. (Courtesy of Earl Abeln.)

In 1963, the Schilling family purchased the Lookout House at 1721 and rebuilt it into a premier location for entertainment and national acts. (Courtesy of Dean Russell and the James A. Ramage Civil War Museum.)

This is a look inside the Lookout House, one of Northern Kentucky's finest nightclubs. (Courtesy of Dean Russell and the City of Fort Wright.)

On the afternoon of August 14, 1973, fire broke out at the Lookout House. The club, which had been closed for two weeks for maintenance, was empty except for a few workers, who all got out safely. The fire caused $2 million in damages and required the help of 10 local fire departments. (Courtesy of Dean Russell and the City of Fort Wright.)

More than 300 spectators came to watch one of the largest fires in Northern Kentucky history as the 80,000-square-foot Lookout House burned down. Dixie Highway was closed for several hours to make room for all the fire trucks and hoses. The smoke, which could be seen for miles, also interrupted nearby I-75 traffic. (Courtesy of Dean Russell and the City of Fort Wright.)

An anchor along Dixie Highway's "Gourmet Strip," Oelsner's Colonial Tavern at 1730 Dixie Highway was five-star dining before there was such a thing as five-star dining. Built in 1937, the restaurant had this photograph taken in the mid-1940s. (Courtesy of Nancy Oelsner Baute.)

In reference to the close proximity of the famed Mason-Dixon Line, the Oelsners named one of the dining rooms the Mason-Dixon Room. Seen in this 1950s photograph are J. Richard Oelsner (left) and Russell Oelsner shaking hands on the line. (Courtesy of Nancy Oelsner Baute.)

This photograph shows Hillcrest Steak House, Jack's Tavern at 1729 Dixie Highway, and the gardens of Oelsner's Colonial Tavern. (Courtesy of Butch Ostendorf.)

The Steffen Farm raised minnows and goldfish near the intersection of Dixie Highway and Sleepy Hollow Road. (Courtesy of Butch Ostendorf.)

This home, built by Fred Lewin around 1925, sat on the northeast corner of Dixie Highway and Kyles Lane until the early 1980s. (Courtesy of Nancy Oelsner Baute.)

The Fred Lewin family lived in the home in the photograph at the top of the page. Seen here are Fredrich, his wife, Mayme Michels Lewin, and their children, Vera, Arthur, and Dolly. (Courtesy of Nancy Oelsner Baute.)

Kuchle Homestead, which was built in 1908, is shown here from Kyles Lane. This is actually the back of the house. The front of the house, which includes a white frame building, was constructed in 1902 and sits behind the Kuchle Garage at 1817 Dixie Highway. (Courtesy of Tom Stamm, Fort Mitchell Garage.)

Joseph Kuchle Horseshoeing, Wagon, and Plow Work at 1817 Dixie Highway is seen in this 1910 photograph. In addition to a blacksmith shop, Kuchle also built wagons for vendors to sell their wares. Shown here is the M. J. Mitchell Daily Meat Market wagon. (Courtesy of Ed and Carol Whitehead.)

The Fort Mitchell–Crescent Springs Ice Delivery Wagon, made by Joseph Kuchle, is seen in this 1910 photograph. Notice the sign advertising the telephone. The Kuchles had one of the few phones in Northern Kentucky at that time. From left to right are (first row) Josepha Kuchle (Joe Kuchle's mother), Marie, Carl, Bertha, Ursula, Helen, Alice, and Joseph Kuchle; (second row) Joe Kuchle Sr. and Gus Elesener. (Courtesy of Ed and Carol Whitehead.)

Shown in 1910, the North College Hill Bakery Wagon was built by Joseph Kuchle. On the goat cart from left to right are Alice, Helen, Ursula, Bertha, Josepha, Joe Jr., and Carl Kuchle. Notice the Kuchle homestead in the background. (Courtesy of Ed and Carol Whitehead.)

Grown men play in a sandbox behind the Kuchle Garage at 1817 Dixie Highway in this 1920s photograph. From left to right are Gus Elesener, Joseph Kuchle Sr., and Carl Kuchle. Across Dixie Highway is Decker Florist. (Courtesy of Ed and Carol Whitehead.)

Kuchle Garage at 1817 Dixie Highway transformed itself from a blacksmith shop into a garage in 1922 as cars became more and more common. (Courtesy of Ed and Carol Whitehead.)

Joseph Kuchle Jr. and his sister Ruth Kuchle (far right) check out the new outdoor lift built for the Kuchle Garage at 1817 Dixie Highway. The rest of girls are unidentified. (Courtesy of Ed and Carol Whitehead.)

Joseph Kuchle Sr. stands with his tow truck outside the Kuchle Garage at 1817 Dixie Highway in this 1948 photograph. (Courtesy of Ed and Carol Whitehead.)

This truck sits near the intersection of Dixie Highway and St. John's Road, which leads to St. John's Cemetery. (Courtesy of Dean Russell and the City of Fort Wright.)

In 1948, the Kuchles added a showroom and started selling cars. They sold Crosley, Tucker, Lincoln, and Mercury automobiles. They also sold cars from the Kaiser-Frazer Corporation, including the Henry J, one of the first compact cars. A brand-new 1948 Crosley with a radio and rearview mirror, which were upgrades, sold for $1,083.86. (Both courtesy of Ed and Carol Whitehead.)

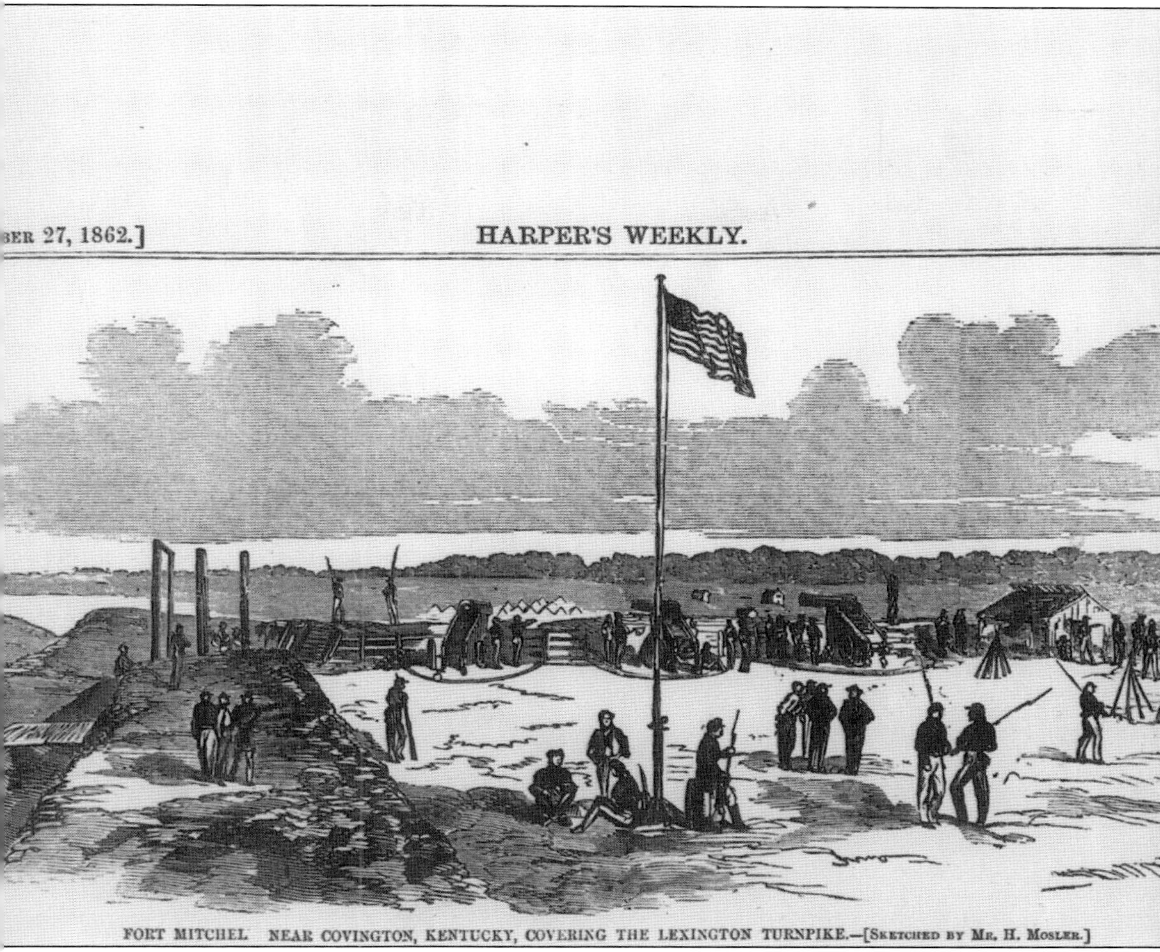

This illustration, seen in *Harper's Weekly* on September 27, 1862, depicts Fort Mitchell, established during the Civil War to guard the north-south artery called the Lexington Turnpike, which later became known as Dixie Highway. The fort, as well as the city, is named after Gen. Ormsby MacKnight Mitchel. The city name, which adds an extra "l" at the end, is actually a misspelling of the general's name. (Courtesy Chester F. Geaslen.)

Shown in this 1940s photograph, Schilling's Drive-In Restaurant at 1939 Dixie Highway was well known for its "Steak and Eggs in a Skillet." (Courtesy of Dean Russell and the City of Fort Wright.)

The Kruempelman Farm stood at the intersection of Ridge Road and Dixie Highway. The home was built in 1893. (Courtesy of Todd Kruempelman.)

Looking north at the intersection of Ridge Road and Dixie Highway, Joseph Foltz works on the Kruempelman Farm in this late-1930s photograph. (Courtesy of Joseph Foltz.)

This view, looking across the same field as the above photograph, was taken about 50 years later from the Kruempelman Farm looking across Dixie Highway to Ames Department Store. (Courtesy of Todd Kruempelman.)

The Foltz homestead stood at the corner of East Orchard Road and Dixie Highway around 1905. (Courtesy of Joseph Foltz.)

St. Agnes School built this new structure around 1940. (Courtesy of Ed and Carol Whitehead.)

The crib scene shown on this 1930s postcard was a tradition at St. Agnes each Christmas. Families would come from all around Northern Kentucky to enjoy it. (Courtesy of Julie Kremer.)

St. Agnes schoolchildren get ready to board the school buses in these early-1950s photographs. (Both courtesy of the Covington Province of the Sisters of Notre Dame.)

This image was taken in the vicinity of Maple Avenue and Dixie Highway, near Green's Grocery, in 1932. (Courtesy of Sheriff Chuck and Ruth Korzenborn.)

This building at 2079 Dixie Highway was home to Kruempelman Realty in the 1990s, but originally it was Green's Grocery, owned by Luke O. Green and his wife, Daisy. The Greens lived upstairs from the grocery, which started in business in the 1930s. The building was torn down when the I-75 exit ramps to Fort Mitchell were redesigned in the early 21st century. (Courtesy of Sheriff Chuck and Ruth Korzenborn.)

Dot Tanner stands near Green's Grocery's Model T delivery truck in 1932 along Dixie Highway in Fort Mitchell. (Courtesy of Sheriff Chuck and Ruth Korzenborn.)

Two people were killed and 28 injured when this Greyhound bus hit the stone pillar at the corner of Dixie Highway and Maple Avenue on May 23, 1944. (Courtesy of Michael J. Fletcher.)

A side view shows Lewin Monuments at 2218 Dixie Highway. This building was constructed in 1959, but the photograph was taken in the 1970s. The photograph also shows a partial view of Robertson's Restaurant next door. (Courtesy of Lewin Monuments.)

Cyril Lewin, who started Lewin Monuments, stands outside the business near 2156 Dixie Highway after a 1940s snowstorm. The business had moved about two blocks south to this location in 1959 to make way for I-75 and a shopping center. (Courtesy of Lewin Monuments.)

Fort Mitchell Baptist Church at 2323 Dixie Highway is seen in this late-1950s photograph. The church has been at this location since June 1, 1924. (Courtesy of Fort Mitchell Baptist Church.)

Blessed Sacrament School is pictured here in the late 1940s. (Courtesy of Lois Ann Shannon.)

The eighth-grade class stands in front of the entrance to Blessed Sacrament School in 1933. (Courtesy of Jeanne Feldhues.)

Blessed Sacrament Church at 2409 Dixie Highway was photographed here around 1950. (Courtesy of Jeanne Feldhues.)

This interior photograph of Blessed Sacrament Church was taken around 1950. (Courtesy of Jeanne Feldhues.)

As the congregation of Blessed Sacrament Church prepared to lay the cornerstone for the new church building, they gathered near Orchard Road and paraded down Dixie Highway to the site. This event took place on May 23, 1920. The school building is behind the trees and the Sisters' House is on the right. (Courtesy of Sheriff Chuck and Ruth Korzenborn.)

The grounds were blessed before the cornerstone was laid. (Courtesy of Sheriff Chuck and Ruth Korzenborn.)

The congregation prayed as the cornerstone was laid. After the service, the men made burgoo and the women served ice cream. (Courtesy of Sheriff Chuck and Ruth Korzenborn.)

This image of a snowstorm looks south on Dixie Highway near the intersection of Dixie and Virginia Avenue in 1904. The tree line in the distance on the left is Orphanage Road. (Courtesy of Tom Stamm, Fort Mitchell Garage.)

Korzenborn Service Station at 2475 Dixie Highway opened in 1935. In this photograph from 1942, Charles G. Korzenborn (left) chats with customer Elmer Hanns. (Courtesy of Sheriff Chuck and Ruth Korzenborn.)

Charles Korzenborn is seen here in front of his service station in 1960. The pretty model is showing off the new Dodge Dart. (Courtesy of Sheriff Chuck and Ruth Korzenborn.)

Members of the Fort Mitchell Volunteer Fire Department, pictured in the winter of 1934, are standing in the area that would soon become the Sunnymede subdivision. The homes in the background are on the south side of Pleasant Ridge Avenue. From left to right are (standing in front of the REO Speedwagon fire truck) Charles Kreutzkamp, Harry Lubke, Henry Schierberg (behind Lubke), Ben Snyder, Charles Frost, Lee Morand (wearing civilian clothes), Ray Becker,

Roy Stokes, Jack Becker, and Al Adrick; (standing in back of the fire truck) George Lubrecht, Karl Hugenberg, Pete Weisenberg, and Gus Adams; (between the cars) Chief John Schroeder (wearing white); (in front of the car) Charles Bogenschultz, George Schrand, and Carl Schmidt; (on the car) Art Schmidt, Herb Flesch, Pop Dye, and Frank Droege. (Courtesy of Sheriff Chuck and Ruth Korzenborn.)

This familiar sight along Dixie Highway in the late 1940s included Toll's Drugs, the 4 Star Dixie Theater (notice Abbott and Costello are showing), and a Kroger store. (Courtesy of Lois Ann Shannon.)

Freihofer Bakery at 2493 Dixie Highway served up hot doughnuts, éclairs, Danish rolls, and Zorro Cookies from 1957 though the early 1980s. (Courtesy of Charles Freihofer.)

This photograph looks north on Dixie Highway at the intersection of Dixie Highway and Orphanage Road in 1957. Remke Markets at 2501 Dixie Highway and Toll's Drugs are just across Orphanage Road. (Courtesy of Remke Markets.)

A streetcar makes the turn at the end of the line in this late-1940s photograph. Notice Greyhound Grill in the background on the right. (Courtesy of Fred Hellmann.)

The Dixie Tea Room, an ice cream shop at 2500 Dixie Highway, opened in 1921. Owner Johnny Hauer sold the business to Al Frisch in the 1930s, and the name changed to the Greyhound Grill. (Courtesy of Arianna Hauer.)

Ramona and Arianna Hauer stand in the Beer Garden of the Dixie Tea Room, at 2500 Dixie Highway, in this late-1930s photograph. (Courtesy of Butch and Mary Ann Wainscott.)

The streetcar and two unidentified streetcar workers are shown near the end of the line in Fort Mitchell in this mid-1950s photograph. Notice the original Fort Mitchell Remke Markets at 2465 Dixie Highway in the background. (Courtesy of Remke Markets.)

Here is the last streetcar to run the line, on July 1, 1950, making the turn at the end of the line near 2500 Dixie Highway. (Courtesy of Wilfrid Hellmann.)

Stevies Roadhouse and Edelweis Gardens opened in 1901 at the corner of Dixie Highway and Horsebranch Road, which is now called Orphanage Road. In later years, it was known as the Kentucky Tavern. (Courtesy of Remke Markets.)

One of Fort Mitchell's first homes, located at the corner of Dixie Highway and Buttermilk Pike, was built by Jacob and Mary Frisch in the early 1900s. In this 1912 photograph, the Frisches are pictured with sons Al (second from left) and Benny (third from left). Benny grew up to own, train, and race greyhounds. Al became a restaurateur, purchasing the Dixie Tea Room at 2500 Dixie Highway in the early 1930s and changing the name to Greyhound Grill in honor of his brother. (Courtesy of Jeanne Feldhues.)

Three

Farther out the Dixie
Lakeside Park, Crestview Hills, and Edgewood

In the late 1800s, this photograph is looking south on Dixie Highway where it intersects I-275 today. (Courtesy of Nancy Oelsner Baute.)

The Kroger home at 2576 Dixie Highway was built in 1923. (Courtesy of June Kohorst Kroger.)

Bernie (left) and Edwin Kroger (right) stand in their front yard at 2576 Dixie Highway in the late 1920s. In the background, one can see their next-door neighbor's house. (Courtesy of June Kohorst Kroger.)

The Krogers' dog Laddie had puppies. Mother Emma Kroger, her sons Edwin (right) and Bernie (left), and a neighbor girl play with them in the front yard of 2576 Dixie Highway around 1930. (Courtesy of June Kohorst Kroger.)

The Kroger boys, Bernie (left) and Edwin (right) are dressed for the cold in this late-1920s photograph. (Courtesy of June Kohorst Kroger.)

Lakeside Park was named for all the lakes in the community. In this photograph, which was taken in the late 1920s, these boys are playing alongside the lake that was behind the Kroger home at 2576 Dixie Highway. (Courtesy of June Kohorst Kroger.)

Looking north on Dixie Highway around 1930, Edwin (left) and Bernie Kroger pose for a photograph in their front yard. (Courtesy of June Kohorst Kroger.)

Mr. and Mrs. Charles Retschulte, seen here in an 1860s photograph, emigrated from Germany and purchased land at 2642 Dixie Highway. They later opened a restaurant on this site. (Courtesy of Mick Cahill.)

Charles Retschulte purchased this tavern at 2642 Dixie Highway in 1910 and in 1912 converted it into a restaurant. Located 5 miles from Covington, the C. Retschulte 5 Mile House was the perfect place to stop to quench the thirst of both horse and rider. This early-1900s photograph was taken on the Fourth of July; Charles is in the middle row with the moustache. (Courtesy of Barleycorn's Five Mile House Restaurant.)

When the Lexington Turnpike was designated a federal highway and renamed the Dixie Highway in 1921, Charles Retschulte renamed his restaurant the Dixie Inn. When the streetcar line was installed, the end of the line was about a mile from his restaurant. Charles, quite the entrepreneur, installed streetlights along the route at his own expense and drove streetcar riders by buggy back and forth to his restaurant. (Courtesy of Barleycorn's Five Mile House Restaurant.)

These well-dressed ladies are enjoying their time at the Dixie Inn in this photograph taken in the 1920s. The owner, Mrs. Retschulte (far left), is next to her granddaughter Florence Retschulte. (Courtesy of Mick Cahill.)

Retschulte Inn, at 2642 Dixie Highway, became a popular gambling spot in the 1940s and 1950s but closed in 1962. After being closed for nine years, Retschulte's was back in operation from 1971 to 1983, as seen in this early-1980s photograph. It reopened as Barleycorn's Five Mile House in 1984. (Courtesy of Barleycorn's Five Mile House Restaurant.)

Appetizers

COMBINATION COCKTAIL	1.25
SHRIMP COCKTAIL	.75
TOMATO JUICE	.15
FILET ANCHOVY	1.00
SOUP	.25

* * *

Dinners

HALF FRIED CHICKEN, Southern Style	2.50
FRESH CHICKEN LIVER, Saute' in Butter	2.75
BROILED HALF GUINEA ON TOAST GARNISHED WITH HAM	3.25
CALF LIVER with BACON or ONIONS	2.75
KENTUCKY-CURED COUNTRY HAM, Natural Gravy	2.75
BROILED LAMB CHOPS (2) With Mint Jelly	3.50
BROILED SIRLOIN STEAK and Fresh Mushrooms	4.00
BROILED FILET MIGNON and Fresh Mushrooms	4.00
DOUBLE SIRLOIN STEAK-for-two and Fresh Mushrooms	8.00

FISH and SEAFOODS

FRENCH FRIED SHRIMP, Tartar Sauce	2.50
FROG LEGS, Tartar Sauce	3.00
FROG LEGS, Saute' in Butter	3.50
BROILED FRESH LAKE TROUT, Butter Sauce	2.75
WHOLE BROILED LIVE LOBSTER with Butter	4.50
AFRICAN LOBSTER TAILS with Drawn Butter	3.50
WHOLE FRESH POMPONO with Almond Butter	3.25
WHOLE FRESH MT. BROOK TROUT with Almond Butter	3.25
BROILED SWORD FISH STEAK with Butter Sauce	2.75

* * *

All meals include setup of relish, celery and olives, cottage cheese, chives, soup, RETSCHULTE'S slaw, choice of two (2) vegetables, potatoes (hash-browned or French-fried), choice of desert, and drink.

A LA CARTE

Sandwiches in Dining Room

HAM	.50
HAM and SWISS CHEESE	1.00
SWISS CHEESE	.50
LIEDERKRANZ	.50

No sandwiches served in dining room after 5:00 P. M.

SOUP	.25
RETSCHULTE DOUBLE-SLAW	.70
RELISH (For One)	.25
COTTAGE CHEESE WITH CHIVES	.25
SLICED TOMATOES	.25

Cheeses

AMERICAN	.50
SWISS	.50
LIEDERKRANZ	.50
ROQUEFORT (Blue)	.50

Served with Bread or Crackers and Butter

Deserts

HOME-MADE PIE	.15
PIE A la MODE	.25
PIE with CHEESE	.25
ICE CREAM	.15
SUNDAE	.25
SHERBET	.15
STRAWBERRY SHORTCAKE	.35
STRAWBERRY SHORTCAKE WITH ICE CREAM	.50

Drinks

COFFEE	.10
POT of TEA	.15
MILK	.15
POSTUM	.15

If your favorite food is not listed, ask your waiter if it is available!

Shown here is the Retschulte Inn menu. (Courtesy of Barleycorn's Five Mile House Restaurant.)

Lakeside Presbyterian Church services were originally held in this white house, owned by the Hill family. The congregation called it the Hill House, located at 2690 Dixie Highway. (Courtesy of Lakeside Presbyterian Church.)

The Lakeside Presbyterian Church building was completed in 1963 in front of the Hill House at 2690 Dixie Highway. (Courtesy of Lakeside Presbyterian Church.)

This view is looking south on Dixie Highway just south of Carran Drive in 1973. (Courtesy of Wilfrid Hellmann.)

This view is looking north on Dixie Highway towards the intersection of Paul Hesser Drive in 1973. (Courtesy of Wilfrid Hellmann.)

Dixie Highway runs through the center of this 1973 photograph. Winding Way Drive is going up the hill on the left side. The house in the center is the Tillman home. (Courtesy of Wilfrid Hellmann.)

From left to right, Joyce, Don, and Joan Hellman stand across the lake from the Tillman home (seen in the above photograph) in 1934. (Courtesy of Butch and Mary Ann Wainscott.)

This is an aerial view of Dixie Heights High School at 3010 Dixie Highway. The school opened in 1936 and was built by the Works Progress Administration. Dixie Highway runs through the center of the photograph, which was taken in the mid-1970s. (Courtesy of the Kenton County Public Library, Covington, Kentucky.)

Heritage International Shopping Center, in the center of this photograph, opened in the late 1970s. (Courtesy of the Kenton County Public Library, Covington, Kentucky.)

Four

Small-Town Charm
Erlanger and Elsmere

To pay for the road, tollgates were installed along the Dixie Highway. Rates were as follows: for each person (except footmen, women, and children under 10 years) 6¢; for each horse or carriage with two wheels, 25¢; for every sleigh, 25¢; for every wagon or carriage with four wheels, 50¢; for every head of meat cattle, 3¢; for every head of hog, sheep, or goat, 1¢. The charge for toll jumping was $10. (Courtesy of Chester F. Geaslen.)

The Kenton Manor Motel was located at 3044 Dixie Highway. On the back of this postcard, it says, "Beautiful Heated Crystal Pool, One of Kentucky's Finest, TV, Background Music, Air Conditioned, Telephone, Playground, Guest Lounge, Colored TV and Restaurant." (Courtesy of Deborah Kohl Kremer.)

Known as the Timberlake Toll Gate, this house was built by William T. Timberlake. Moving into the Erlanger area in the 1820s, Timberlake was very active in community affairs and influential in the establishment of the Covington-Lexington Turnpike. (Courtesy of the Kenton County Public Library, Covington, Kentucky.)

Chinatown and Foodmart were new in 1965. Chinatown, located at 3135 Dixie Highway, was one of the largest discount department stores in the Midwest. Foodmart, at 3129 Dixie Highway, was open from 9:00 a.m. to 9:00 p.m., which was a new concept at that time. (Courtesy of the Kenton County Public Library, Covington, Kentucky.)

This early-1980s photograph is looking south on Dixie Highway near 3104 Dixie Highway. (Courtesy of Matthew Kenney.)

Shown here is an aerial view of the Roundup Club at 3100 Dixie Highway, at the intersection of Dixie Highway and Kenton Lands Road. The popular nightclub was established in 1965 and closed in 1981. (Courtesy of Matthew Kenney.)

This Dixie Highway view of the Roundup Club is complete with stagecoach and covered wagon. They also kept a live caged bear on the premises in the 1970s. (Courtesy of Matthew Kenney.)

The Roundup Club had a pool out back where kids could come on weekend afternoons, or bar patrons could use it in the evenings. (Courtesy of Matthew Kenney.)

This interior view of the Roundup Club includes Gene Kenney, the owner of the club. Notice the log cabin and barred windows, which gave it the feel of the Old West. (Courtesy of Matthew Kenney.)

The Roundup Club had quite a collection of unique items inside this popular night spot. In this photograph, they are delivering a round safe, weighing 8,000 pounds, which was acquired from Hebron Deposit Bank. (Courtesy of Matthew Kenney.)

The Cabana Restaurant opened at 3126 Dixie Highway in 1948. It was operated by Stella Montgomery and her daughter and son-in-law, John W. and Leah Montgomery Fletcher. (Courtesy of Michael J. Fletcher.)

The interior photograph features the main bar and dining room of the Cabana Restaurant in 1948. (Courtesy of Michael J. Fletcher.)

In 1952, Stella Montgomery decided to add a second floor for a banquet room above the main dining room and a 12-lane bowling alley in the back. (Courtesy of Michael J. Fletcher.)

The banquet room was called the Highway Room. (Courtesy of Michael J. Fletcher.)

The Montgomerys added a sign to the roof to advertise the Kenton Lanes Bowling Alley, but everyone still referred to it, and the restaurant, as the Cabana. (Courtesy of Michael J. Fletcher.)

The Kenton Lanes Bowling Alley was so successful that in just a few years they added six more lanes. (Courtesy of Michael J. Fletcher.)

Herb Rolsen Boats and Motors moved from Covington to 3130 Dixie Highway in the late 1950s. The sign was visible from Dixie Highway, but the business was behind the Cabana. As a Johnson Outboard Motor dealer, Herb Rolsen attached a plastic replica of an outboard motor to his 1952 Plymouth and used it to advertise his business. (Courtesy of Michael J. Fletcher.)

Pictured here is the interior of Herb Rolsen Boats and Motors in the late 1950s. The building originally housed a newspaper publisher, who had built a large pit in the floor to hold the printing press. When Rolsen moved in, he decided to fill this pit with water and display a boat there. His ingenuity earned him some publicity; the showroom was featured in a boating industry magazine. (Courtesy of Michael J. Fletcher.)

Johnny's Car Wash at 3152 Dixie Highway opened for business in 1965. This photograph was taken in 1966. Notice the huge burley tobacco warehouse behind the car wash. (Courtesy of Jeff Simpson.)

Johnny's Car Wash is pictured at 3152 Dixie Highway in this early-1970s photograph. (Courtesy of Jeff Simpson.)

The original Colonial Cottage Restaurant, located at 3140 Dixie Highway, operated from 1933 to 1987. They still serve up Southern-style home-cooking at their new location on adjacent property. Their address is still 3140 Dixie Highway. (Courtesy of Matt Grimes.)

The house on the right is located at 3307 Dixie Highway and is the home of Wilfrid Hellmann in this late-1930s photograph. (Courtesy of Wilfrid Hellmann.)

This was the view from the driveway of 3307 Dixie Highway prior to the building of the railroad underpass. Railroad tracks crossed Dixie Highway just in front of the walker on the left side of the photograph. (Courtesy of Wilfrid Hellmann.)

Emma Hellmann stands in her driveway at 3307 Dixie Highway alongside her 1935 Terraplane car, which was manufactured by the Hudson Motor Car Company. (Courtesy of Wilfrid Hellmann.)

The view here is looking north on Dixie Highway as construction started for the Southern Railroad underpass in 1937. Readers can see the Erlanger Railroad Depot and Erlanger Lumber on the left. On right side of photograph, Joseph Herrmann is peeking out of a ditch. (Courtesy of Wilfrid Hellmann.)

Shown here is the digging of the Southern Railroad underpass in 1937. (Courtesy of Wilfrid Hellmann.)

Here is another 1937 view of workers digging the Southern Railroad underpass. (Courtesy of Wilfrid Hellmann.)

In this 1960 photograph looking south on Dixie Highway, the intersection of Donaldson Road (Route 236) and Dixie is on the right and Stevenson Road and Dixie is on the left. (Courtesy of Fred Hellmann.)

The front of Joseph G. Herrmann's Grocery in 1909 is pictured here. The store was on the east side of Dixie Highway, just south of Stevenson Road. (Courtesy of Fred Hellmann.)

June Kohorst, with her aunt, Madeline Nead, is in the front yard at 9 Commonwealth Avenue in this 1942 photograph. In the background, the cars are on Dixie Highway, with Commonwealth on the left. The building on the left is Bentler Drugs. (Courtesy of June Kohorst Kroger.)

Angie Brake Wilmhoff (left), Stanley "Snorkey" Douba (center), and June Kohorst are near the corner of Garvey Avenue and Dixie Highway in 1941. (Courtesy of June Kohorst Kroger.)

The Community Bank building, located near 3420 Dixie Highway, was constructed around 1912 as the Citizens Bank Building. In 1914, a free public library opened in a room of the building, offering 300 books. The Great Depression brought the demise of the bank, and Erlanger did not have a bank for nearly five years. On February 15, 1936, longtime Erlanger resident Andy Sheben Sr. opened the Community Bank in the former Citizens Bank Building. (Courtesy of Kathy DeZarn.)

The intersection of Dixie Highway and Garvey Avenue is seen in this 1970s photograph. Across the street is Dixie Dry Goods, a popular clothing store. (Courtesy of the Kenton County Public Library, Covington, Kentucky.)

The wedding of Art Kremer and Marge Domaschko is pictured here on November 24, 1949, at St. Henry Church, 3813 Dixie Highway. (Courtesy of Kathy DeZarn, Connie Fry, Linda Morehead, and Art, Larry, Ken, and Tim Kremer.)

Several members of the graduating class of 1943 of St. Henry High School pose in front of their school building. The class had 19 graduates. From left to right are (girls) June Kohorst Kroger, Rosemary Cahill Mathis, and Angela Brake Wilmhof; (boys) Harry Nussbaum, Bob Hoffman, Dick Klaine, Ronald Rosing, and Gus Wessling. (Courtesy of June Kohorst Kroger.)

St. Henry School's First Communicants of 1927 line up for their photograph on the porch of the nuns' house, adjacent to the school and church. (Courtesy of Kathy DeZarn.)

A highlight of the menu of the Swan Restaurant at 4311 Dixie Highway was Swan's Mixed Grilled Plate. It came with a "Pork Chop, Chopped Tenderloin Steak Pattie, Breaded Veal Cutlet with Tomato Sauce, Grilled Tomato, and Mixed Salad with Roquefort Dressing and Rolls with Butter," all for $1.75. (Courtesy of Dave Schreiver.)

In 1955, the Swan Restaurant closed abruptly. The building sat abandoned for one year until Albert Joseph Schreiver purchased it as a new home for his florist business. When Swan Florist opened in the Swan Restaurant in 1956, all of the furnishings from the restaurant were still inside the building. In this photograph, Albert Joseph Schreiver Sr. (right) poses amid his new floral display tables, which used to be dining room tables. Notice the carved wooden swans that create the crown molding near the ceiling and the former booths on the left side of the photograph, now accommodating small nooks for floral displays. (Courtesy of Dave Schreiver.)

When Albert Joseph Schreiver Sr. purchased the old Swan Restaurant, he kept the name and the sign because everyone already knew it as the Swan. (Courtesy of Dave Schreiver.)

In this 1958 photograph, Charles Lunsford (left) and Albert Joseph Schreiver Sr. (right) pose in front of Swan Florist at 4311 Dixie Highway. (Courtesy of Dave Schreiver.)

This aerial photograph of Dixie Highway and Swan Florist was taken in the late 1970s. (Courtesy of Dave Schreiver.)

The back of this postcard from Doc's Place, at 4442 Dixie Highway, reads, "The good home-cooked food and reasonable prices at Doc's Place is the reason it has become a favorite eating place of the tourist from every state, traveling U.S. 25 and U.S. 42 out of Cincinnati, Ohio." (Courtesy of Deborah Kohl Kremer.)

Five

THE U.S. 25 AND U.S. 42 SPLIT
FLORENCE AND BOONE COUNTY

These children and their goat cart are believed to be standing on Dixie Highway in Florence in 1914. This photograph depicts many things that have changed with the times: the unpaved road, the barefoot boy, and the boy on the right who appears to be smoking. (Courtesy of Chester F. Geaslen.)

The home of Carl and Pearl Anderson at 6614 Dixie Highway is seen in the early 1960s. This home, which still stands today, has been added on to and converted from a private residence to a business, but the architectural beauty can still be seen. (Courtesy of the Fitzgerald Collection, Boone County Public Library.)

Right next door to their home, Pearl Anderson and her daughter Alice started Family Garden Flower Shop at 6616 Dixie Highway. This photograph was taken in 1961. (Courtesy of the Fitzgerald Collection, Boone County Public Library.)

The Albers store, opening in 1959 at the corner of Dixie Highway and Turfway Road, was a welcome addition to Florence. In this photograph, Mr. and Mrs. Roy Lutes enjoy the grand opening. The store, called a supermarket, was beloved for their S&H Green Stamps, which shoppers could collect and redeem for luggage, knife sets, and other exciting household items. (Courtesy of the Fitzgerald Collection, Boone County Public Library.)

The opening of the new Albers store must have been big news at the time. Notice the giant WCPO-TV camera in the parking lot. (Courtesy of the Fitzgerald Collection, Boone County Public Library.)

Standing on Dortha Avenue, which was a dirt road in the early 1930s, is little Irwin Carpenter. He is standing right near the intersection of Dortha and Dixie Highway. (Courtesy of the Fitzgerald Collection, Boone County Public Library.)

Southern Trails Restaurant, seen in this 1961 photograph, was a popular family-style restaurant located at 6823 Dixie Highway. Southern Trails was well-known for their fried chicken dinners. (Courtesy of the Fitzgerald Collection, Boone County Public Library.)

Looking north on Dixie Highway, Southern Trails Restaurant proclaimed they were Boone County's most popular meeting place. They offered banquet rooms and catering and apparently the option of outdoor dining. (Courtesy of the Fitzgerald Collection, Boone County Public Library.)

Florence Motel, also known as Florence Motor Court, located at 7111 Dixie Highway, is seen in this early-1960s photograph. Old postcards describe it as "23 Modern Rooms, Tile Showers, Air Conditioning, Television and a Radio. Just 10 Miles from downtown Cincinnati OH." (Courtesy of the Fitzgerald Collection, Boone County Public Library.)

The Florence Christian Church, which is located at the southern corner of Main Street and U.S. 42, where Dixie Highway splits from U.S. 42, is seen in 1960. This church has been conducting services on this site since 1830. (Courtesy of the Fitzgerald Collection, Boone County Public Library.)

Caintuckee Grill was a popular hangout on the north corner of the intersection of Dixie Highway and Main Street from the 1950s to 1984. It was frequented by local politicians, and many plans were put into motion over a cup of coffee and an order of eggs sunny-side up. The Cain family, who started the restaurant, created the name by combining their name and "Kentucky." (Courtesy of the Fitzgerald Collection, Boone County Public Library.)

The highway marker for the Skirmish at Florence, located at the intersection of U.S. 25, U.S. 42, and Main Street, is barely visible among all the other signs and advertising in this 1961 photograph. On September 17, 1862, the Confederate army traveled north along the Lexington Turnpike toward Cincinnati. They were met at this location by the Union army, and a skirmish broke out. One Union soldier, five Confederate soldiers, and one civilian were killed in the conflict. (Courtesy of the Fitzgerald Collection, Boone County Public Library.)

Skyline Drive-In, on the eastern corner of the intersection of U.S. 25 and U.S. 42, says on their sign they are famous for good food. These early-1960s photographs show that both the Elsmere and Florence Police Department must have thought so, too. (Both courtesy of the Fitzgerald Collection, Boone County Public Library.)

Dixie Motor Court Motel and Restaurant, at 8485 Dixie Highway, opened in April 1948. Owned by Curtis Ely, it was famous for the Kentucky-shaped sign out front. The motel transformed itself into efficiency apartments in the 1960s with the opening of I-75, which rerouted the traffic away from Dixie Highway. (Courtesy of Judi Deathridge.)

Florence Drive-In, located just south of the Dixie Highway and Turfway Road intersection, opened May 22, 1947. The drive-in, which could host 800 cars, entertained Northern Kentucky residents for almost five decades, showing everything from Disney's *Herbie the Love Bug* to the Cheech and Chong movies of the 1970s and 1980s. The Florence, as locals called it, closed for good in 1988. (Courtesy of the Fitzgerald Collection, Boone County Public Library.)

The interior of the Southern Trails Restaurant is shown in this undated postcard. On the back, it says, "Famous for our extravagant Sunday Salad Buffet & Family Style Dinner." (Courtesy of Deborah Kohl Kremer.)

The Ridge Motel at 6501 Dixie Highway operated from 1963 to 1970. The back of this postcard says, "Featuring 22 units with air conditioning, hot water heat, televisions and telephones." (Courtesy of Deborah Kohl Kremer.)

Rainbo Cabins, also known as Rainbo Tourist Homes, at 6710 Dixie Highway, was a popular stop for travelers. It was located near the corner of Dixie Highway and Goodridge Avenue. (Courtesy of the Fitzgerald Collection, Boone County Public Library.)

John Powers and Henry Carpenter are pictured at a blacksmith shop on the corner of Dixie Highway and Maher Road. The men appear to be blacksmiths, but it looks like they also made wagon wheels. Notice the flyer on the right advertising the Erlanger Fair, which took place August 19–22, 1907. This fair was a big deal, complete with livestock shows, dancers, palm readers, and refreshments. (Courtesy of Boone County Public Library.)

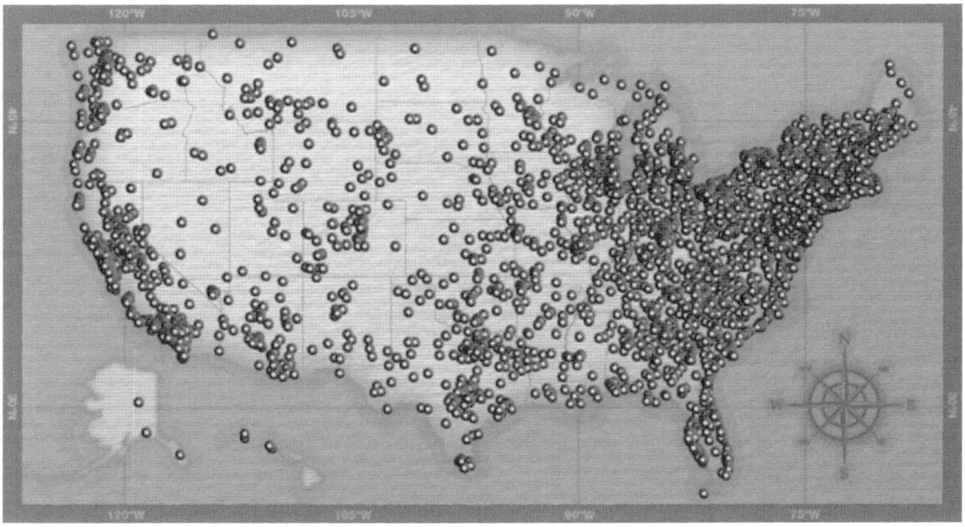